Andrew ✵ Safa

Carmen ● Robert ● Jaclynn 🍎

Cesar A. ✴ Kenna ✓ Carlos ★

Shana ☀ Tiffany ♥ Miriam

Rajesh

by

Curt & Gita Kaufman

With Photographs by

Curt Kaufman

ATHENEUM 1985 NEW YORK

JE

c.1

To P.S. 166 — where it all worked.

Special thanks to:
Prof. Helen Boehm,
Marcia Marshall, Jerome Coopersmith...
and Cele

ISBN 0-689-31074-9
Copyright © 1985 by Curt and Gita Kaufman
All rights reserved
Published simultaneously in Canada by
Collier Macmillan Canada Inc.
Text set by Linoprint Composition, New York City
Printed and bound by Maple-Vail, Binghamton, New York
Designed by Mary Ahern
First Edition

CL
JUL   '86

My name is Rajesh. That means "prince."

Here I am dressing for my first day in school. I was scared the other children would make fun of me because of my legs and hand. As I pulled my pants on over my prostheses, I wished I didn't have to go.

Prostheses are plastic legs. The hospital made them for me so I could walk. I need them to walk because my *own* legs aren't very good.

No one knows why, but when I was born my legs and my right hand weren't all there.

Mommy and Daddy wanted me to go to regular school to learn and to play with regular children.

I was afraid because I didn't want the other boys and girls to laugh at me. That makes me unhappy, and sometimes I want to cry.

At school the teacher asked me my name, and I said, "My name is Rajesh."

Then Mommy *had* to leave. "Don't go," I cried. "I love you!" "I love you, too," Mommy answered. She kissed me and was gone. She had to go to work.

I went to the
blocks and played
with the big airplane
by myself.

I played the piano by myself for a while.

Then a girl with pompoms in her hair
came over.

She looked at my hand.

I looked at her because her pompoms
were so pretty.

I wanted to be her friend.

She smiled, and we played piano
together.

We saw the other children pretending
to be little deer with antlers.

I watched and tried it too. I put my
hands up, and I was a tall reindeer.

Some of the children made
pictures of themselves.
Shanequa was coloring a picture
of herself. It's hard to make pompoms.

When I sewed my name, I wished I
had a real hand.

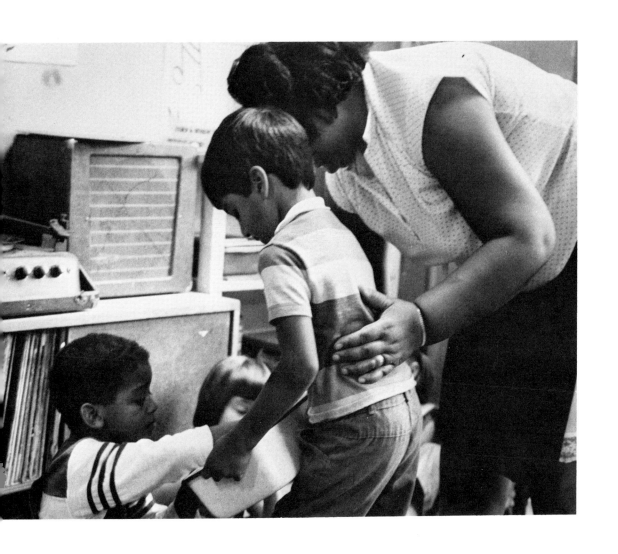

Then I passed out the cookies.

At recess I hung on the bars.

Some bigger kids pulled up my pants and saw my legs. They said, "Why are your legs funny? How did they get like that?"

They were *laughing* at me.

I said, "I was born that way," and my hands let go.

I ran to the slide to play with my friend Shanequa.

Mommy visited the next day, while I told the class about my legs, called prostheses.

I told the class how happy Mommy and Daddy and I were when the doctor said I could walk with my new legs, and I could wear my new sneakers.

Now, I would not always have to be in a wheelchair.

After I finished, Kenna wanted to talk
too. She showed everybody her loose tooth.

Then we danced and sang, "If you're
happy and you know it..."

Remy asked me to play house. I would be the father, and she would be the mommy. I guess she likes me, too.

Spring came, and I was growing.

I was absent one day because I was in the hospital where they made me some bigger legs.

When I came back, we talked about "Different." What would it be like if everyone in the class were the same?

Clara said, "It would be boring; you would see the same face, even if someone was missing."

Andrew said,
"You couldn't make
lots of friends. You
could only make
Rajesh."

Shanequa said,
"Being different, it's
really good because if
it's all Rajeshes, you
couldn't find out who
was who—*and* you
couldn't even find
the *real* Rajesh!"

We celebrated
all summer birthdays
at one time. My
birthday is in the
summer—August
27th. The class made
me a birthday card.
Everyone signed it.

Our teacher let me take a picture on her camera by myself. The pictures come out right away.

I took a picture of Sara, and Sara took a picture of me.

Sara showed me the picture she made, and I showed her the one I made.

It's the last day of school. The weather is hot and sticky. Our teacher said we could put on our bathing suits and go to the sprinklers.

I thought my friends might still make fun of my legs. But I went outside and ran around under the water anyway. It felt nice and cool! All the kids were running and laughing under the sprinklers.

No one stared at my legs, and *no one* made fun of me!

Later we went inside and made music together.

The class played "Row, Row, Row Your Boat." We *all* made one big boat.

Sara and I shook the tambourines. I shook harder and harder to make everyone sing louder and louder and more beautifully.

School is over too soon.
But now I can read.
I can play.
I can go to school.
I can make new friends.
I can *do* almost anything anyone else
can *do!* I am *Rajesh!!*